Dedications

To everyone in the imagination; that is where we all are after all.

I call my Heaven—Toucanaeloka so I offer this book to all the Toucanaelokans who are already there; 150,000,000 angels. Cheers Princess Grace Kelly and Jimi Hendrix 110%.

Special dedication to Mum and Dad, the whole family and all my Anam Cara.

One more mention to my one true Love, Princess Panacea, I love you.

Mishmashaton

CHAOS PHYSICS 42

AUSTIN MACAULEY PUBLISHERS®
LONDON * CAMBRIDGE * NEW YORK * SHARJAH

Copyright © Jason Christopher McLean (Mishmashaton) 2025

The right of Jason Christopher McLean aka Mishmashaton to be identified as author of this work has been asserted by the author in accordance with sections 77 and 78 of the Copyright, Designs and Patents Act 1988.

All rights reserved. No part of this publication may be reproduced, stored in a retrieval system, or transmitted in any form or by any means, electronic, mechanical, photocopying, recording, or otherwise, without the prior permission of the publishers.

Any person who commits any unauthorised act in relation to this publication may be liable to criminal prosecution and civil claims for damages.

A CIP catalogue record for this title is available from the British Library.

ISBN 9781035864270 (Paperback)
ISBN 9781035864287 (ePub e-book)

www.austinmacauley.com

First Published 2025
Austin Macauley Publishers Ltd®
1 Canada Square
Canary Wharf
London
E14 5AA

Acknowledgements

Krishna, Buddha, Jesus, Muhammad and Heavenly Father Jehovah are the main players I would like to thank for the opportunity to create another book for you all. After the modest success of *Little White Teeth* it is hoped that this effort will gain a higher level of attainment. If the previous book was a D then maybe this one can be granted an A*.

Key note speakers who played a part in the making of this humble book are: Audrey Hepburn, Professor Sigmund Freud, Albert Einstein (E = mc2), Bruce Lee (sensei of thoughts), Sir Winston Churchill (Nobel Prize for Literature) the cat next door, many friends (mentioning no names), family near and far and finally all the dream lovers around the world who have been lovable and kind-hearted to Mishmashaton over the last four years.

Foreword

Jason A.K.A. Mishmashaton is my son and author of the book *Chaos Physics 42*. When he asked me to write the foreword, I felt honoured and privileged to do so. By shedding some insight on the author, you will come to know him better and how it all began. As you explore the first few pages you will notice that he has travelled quite a bit in his earlier years, starting with my homeland of Belize in Central America. Jason was born in Hampshire, England, and it was 1981, our first home, but moved quite a lot thereafter. I longed for sunny days in Belize but was so happy in England with my new family and first-born son. As a new mother, I had no idea of the risk of having a 'blue baby' but was grateful we both survived the trauma that was then. I am proud to be Jason's mum, and that he has not given up his writing even when he faces many struggles and seeks to find meaning in life to overcome them. This collection of his work will captivate you as it has me. There are verses which are deep and emotional, and others elegantly simplistic that exudes warmth and joy as he expresses himself effortlessly through his work. At times of stress and chaos, he finds the light in the nibs of his pens, when sleep is hard to achieve, and the nights are long. If you are reading this book, I hope it will offer you motivation and inspiration to never give up on your dreams as you are the owner of your destiny.

As time went by, Jason's brother Michael was born, and our family was complete. His father travelled to work where he was posted to, as he served in the British Forces. Countries such as: Uganda, Nepal, Germany, Ireland, USA, Sharjah, Hong Kong, Belize and we sometimes went with him as allowed, but also travelled for fun to many faraway lands. Jason always explored the outdoors, joining in: swimming, football, rugby, athletics and engaged in clubs and later in The Duke of Edinburgh Award Scheme, when he became more interested in mountain climbing and charity work. However, as a family every night we read with the boys, taking it in turns to listen to each other read. One particular book that was inspirational was *Aesop's Fables* and was a delight to explore and learn together. Many other books including the children's *Encyclopaedia Brittanica*, the children's Bible stories, Roald Dahl books and Dick King-Smith collections, and the *Mr Men* and *Little Miss* books… Jason loved to collect magazines such as *Beano*, *Dandy* and *Buster* and would always get the Christmas annuals. Our house was and still is full of books as his father is a voracious reader, and Jason finds any occasion to buy him another book.

Nepal, Germany, Belize and Texas, hold the fondest memories of Jason's early childhood, firstly, when we lived in Nepal and he learnt to horse ride, enjoyed many outdoor pursuits, but also was often chosen to narrate at the school performances because Jason was already a competent and fluent reader at age 7 years old. Visiting the Americas to spend time with family and swimming in the Caribbean Sea were highlights of the adventurous Jason. He would write to his family, often in a poetic format and his writing developed over the years. Living in Germany gave us opportunities to travel on the continent and as a big brother to Michael, he would point out trees and say, 'Michael, look, Australia is over there!' to which Michael's response was always, 'Where?' and everyone would burst into laughter, which also happened when he retold the event at Michael's wedding (Jason is now uncle to three beautiful nieces).

It is with passion that Jason chose to study Sports and Exercise Science at degree level, after his sporting abilities whilst at boarding school in Kent which continued at Sixth Form in Colchester. However, sadly whilst at university in Sheffield he became unwell and his first breakdown changed the path of his life. Writing became a therapeutic tool, and he resumed his studies a year later and completed his degree, home in Colchester. Jason had only just turned 20 years old when he was diagnosed with Bipolar Affective Disorder and as much as it has often given him the energy to write non-stop, it has robbed him of many opportunities in recent years. He bounces back and reaches out for help from his family, friends and the community, but also enjoys films and listening to the radio. Writing helps Jason to express himself, his feelings, and his thoughts, sometimes it's for other people, and sometimes it's for our ancestors or as an outlet of his creative energy. I hope that you the reader will gain some insight as to why Jason writes as he does, and by purchasing his book it will help him to realise that he has many stories to tell which can help and inspire others. I see and feel Jason's love for others as he greets and includes people he knows and doesn't know, the way he smiles and shares with others and puts them first. It's been an extremely difficult time presently for Jason – I as his mother know he will overcome the challenges through faith and love. We love you Jase, and wish you all good health and joy in this next phase, moving forwards with *Chaos Physics 42*.

Lastly not my words, but another, 'Love has never been too far from the author with a steady string of silver threads from around 1997AD until more recently. Hey, there are over seven billion people on the planet, someone for everyone, right? Mishmashaton knows he will find the Golden thread one day unless he has already found her and not fully realised it yet in the truest sense of the word; in other words, he does believe 'Omnia Vincet amor', 'Love Conquers Everything'.

Jason hopes you will like this latest collection; it is something of a baby so please do not be too harsh on him. Anyway, take care and remember 'Carpe Diem', Seize the Day'.

Mishmashaton

Born: Friday 10:31am, 6th February 1981 Star Sign: Aquarius Chinese Zodiac: Rooster

Timeline of where Mishmashaton lived...

Hampshire England (1981-1986)

Dharan Nepal (1986-1988)

Dusseldorf and Birgelen, Germany (1988-1992)

Colchester, England (1992–2025)

Places visited include:

The Americas-Belize (Ambregis Caye, Caye Caulker), Guatemala, Honduras, Mexico, USA. Asia- India, Nepal, Thailand. Europe: Austria, Belgium, Denmark, France, Germany, Isle of Wight, Italy, Luxembourg, Malta, Netherlands, Scotland, Slovenia, Spain, Switzerland, Tenerife and Wales.

Table of Contents

Book 1: "Quantum Kinetic Liebestraum"   13

    1. Honey Drop Song   15

    2. Calmness in Motion   16

    3. Run with Your Shadow   17

    4. Posturing Photon   18

    5. Summum Bonum   19

    6. As the Wind Blows   20

    7. Weeding For Eden   21

    8. As Life Becomes Heaven   22

    9. Love Drops   23

    10. Stay Awakened   25

    11. Something out of Nothing   27

    12. Liebestraum   31

Book 2: Ruminations   33

Book 3: Journey to Eternity   39

Book 4: Smashed And Rebuilt A—Z Z—A   45

Book 1
"Quantum Kinetic Liebestraum"

"(Small Motions towards Loves Dream)"

1. Honey Drop Song

Bee in a steady state flight,
To be a bee,
See right sight to see a busy bee,
Hive for site to live like bees,
Stings a fright to be a stinging bee,
Upon a wave,
Wind on wings,
Upon a stave,
Honey drops in,
To satisfy a queen bee,
As the swarm sings,
Each wing merrily beats,
To the honey drop song of bees,
To the honey drop song of bees.

(The author wishes he was more musical then perhaps there would be a melody to go with the words written. Originally, the above verse was titled 'Psalm for a Bumble Bee' and scribbled on a bus ticket; the piece only took 15 minutes to create, which is the length of the journey. Unfortunately, the ticket has since disappeared.)

2. Calmness in Motion

Little by little, the butterfly appeared,
Edged out of close, chrysalis, cocoon,
In a land often called neither here nor there,
One beaming, balmy, bright afternoon.

Flowers, bush, bush, flowers, scripted scrolls, sky blue,
Low, high, high, low as mood built anew,
Near a path in a field omnipresent so we knew,
Flowers, bush, bush, flowers, scripted scrolls were nature's truth.

Fluttering by, the butterfly bounced,
Amazingly near a maze of pollen,
Streams of cakelike icing tops,
Hive thieves politely kept 'n' stolen.

One beaming, balmy, bright afternoon,
Moments to capture raising the mood,
Placing hue in a trancelike glare,
Summer sunshine, sublime, so rare.

Ways suiting praise, forward floating, gentle flaps, no obvious pain,
Up to the breeze and the waves of the trees,
Brilliant beauty remember the name…
Brimstone Butterfly.

3. Run with Your Shadow

Run with your shadow,

It will never leave even if you try.

Run with your shadow,

It will never leave even if you try.

The night reveals your shadow.

When the sun arrives, your shadow stays.

Run with your shadow,

Night and day.

4. Posturing Photon

In space, the place was dark until the appearance of the 'All Knowing' stance.

Permission granted for a quantum kinetic performance dance.

Posturing photon never knew what could happen if the light shone through.

As a particle piece, the photon flew.

Red Dwarf ideas and quasars,

Wormholes to dig,

Space manifesting sparks so big like lasers,

Smashing force with the source of all love and light.

"There's eternity to resolve!" said the Great, Great Might!

"So here's to kinetic dreamtime tonight," uttered the son in a lofty height.

"The posturing photon did all right this day of cosmic creation."

5. Summum Bonum

(Highest Good)

Shalom, Shalom, Summum Bonum,
Forever-pleasing smiles,
As we face all questing trials,
As we face all testing trials,
Eternal life with cheers to guide,
Summum Bonum, Summum Bonum,
Journeying, enjoying rides,
Shalom, Shalom, Shalom,
We ask for pleasant patience, please,
Precision here in ways of ease,
We hear, clear clarity, in heaven's pleasing peace,
Summum Bonum, Shalom, Shalom,
Summum Bonum, Shalom.

6. As the Wind Blows

(Renewables)

Invisible forces blowing strong,
Wind pushes blades as only she can,
Generating much from the gentlest touch,
Her presence is welcome in the world.

A rotor spins, the wind blows,
Beginning and ending in one swift move,
Towards spirit and nature's victory groove,
Saving a forest of trees,
Humankind at level infinity,
As the wind blows displaying divinity.

As the wind blows,
As the wind blows,
As the wind blows,
As the wind blows.

7. Weeding For Eden

Fallen leaves achieve their peace,
The trees relieve their seasoned grief,
Gardens cropped to please a chief,
Land filled with flowers, scenes so brief,
Man battles against the weedy thief,
Grappling for nourishment in the soil,
Hours spent pulling out wild plants with toil,
Some place the nettles in a pot to boil,
Oh, how weeds wreck and spoil,
The beauty in a garden's soil,
Roses appear next to thorns,
Mini devils locking horns,
Subtle scents since the day they were born,
Mother Earth's clothes worn,
In a garden with earth to churn,
Winters freeze; summers burn,
Once the seeds are put in place,
Rays and droplets on the go,
Quantum ecology in full flow.

8. As Life Becomes Heaven

Time passes by, youth to old age,
Adventures are memories, a quality gauge,
Musing takes place, feet up on a stool,
Dark locks to grey fox,
Now wise, was cool,
Reviewing the scenes in a worn head,
Closer to the end than birth, soon dead,
Forgotten people once good friends,
Only a handful survived; benevolent blends,
No enemy to battle but the trickling of years,
Steady emotion replaces painful tears,
Here's to forever and eternal life,
Created; a family, children, love for a wife,
Onwards to heaven, feet will march on,
Riches in virtue, big heart so strong,
On the brink of a flat line monitor says soon,
No more adoring the glowing full moon,
Ancient yet playful, all full of cheer,
Preparing a song for the angels to hear,
Last breath taken, family look on with a smile,
A pillar has fallen to rise in a while,
Greeted by saints and mates at the gate,
No more wondering, the end of a wait,
Great Spirit chooses our outcome from here,
With respect and love, there is nothing to fear.

9. Love Drops

Words in air speak volumes to one and to all,
A sentiment is often small.
Two lives becoming one,
A life together like a song.
Where there is love,
There is nothing so strong!
Love can glue hearts together,
Connect sacred souls,
Unravel mysteries, it rocks, it rolls.
Happiness is inside the heart of love.
Love is beautiful, never ugly; soul beauty is eternal.
Love can create ordinary miracles.
The heart knows what love is.
Love exists in the mind of man for everyone who truly believes it can; love is good.
Faith and friendship are the vehicles that drive communities.
Be warm as temperate can be or not to be lukewarm.
Love is measured in happy experiences; find your form and secretly dance.
When love enters the heart strings, music begins to play a symphony of devotion.
Sentiment is to cement love; tokens are easily forgotten.
Love is subtle; love is blind; love is a precious gem to find that is mined.
Heaven is freedom; the journey is testing,
Without love on your side, there is no time for resting.
A bride is beauty, her groom a gent,
Love is unity in oneness content.

Happiness comes to the one who mostly loves!

The owl is wise; the lion is courageous,

Truth is a mate for life; tigers are dangerous.

Higher virtue comes from friendships that are sincere.

Heaven is for lovers of peace, love and understanding; it is in absolute truth that all the

Mysteries are unravelled; it does not have to be demanding.

Of all the places to find love, seek it with a smile.

Look not for approval in the process of life; instead, find happiness in every opportunity and passing seconds.

Above all gifts, love is the purest; it comes from heaven and is truer than a life of selfishness.

Blessed is he who finds love freely; seek and ye shall find.

Kindness is like gold – precious and valuable.

One love in one vision in a vision of one love is all you need to satisfy a million hungry souls.

Swords may clash and words may fly,

In the quest for true love.

If you find it, hold on tight,

Like a stalactite that never dies.

Friends listen; friends care,

Friends are open; friends share.

Life is very short; there is no time for misery.

Look far enough inwards, and you will see heavenly glory.

10. Stay Awakened

Experienced by trial and error, the journey to eternity is a story of awakening and dreaming.

There are voices following me around.

Sometimes I feel that they may be angels,

That would be so so cool!

Worry not, the time is now!

'Time for what…?' I hear the thought.

Be aware today.

If divinity asks no question, living is to affirm the Spirit.

Discover yourself; feel the fear.

Transform what is far into something near.

Nothing evil lasts for eternity; be strong!

All the misery in the world equals pain!

You are not your pain! What is the time?

Half-past nine

Spiders crawl innocently enough,

Then one walks past you, showing off.

Man is standing beside the fire…

Excite with personality

Stun with a love that never dies,

After a moment, smile and leave as friends; foe no more

Sweetness of nature always finds a home.

A sweet home is a hive of honey.

Where there is a honey, be sweet.

Beasts are small, great, gentle and wild.

Children are small and gentle.

Great and wild is life untamed.

Peace can be found in a nutshell.

If you like happy nuts, dose yourself up.

Nutshells litter a squirrel's layer 'Tidy-up time!'

Spiritual truth is common sense.

Common is for everyone,

This truth is a 'simple observation'.

Fools eat all day and still hunger

Wise ones are more subtle…

11. Something out of Nothing

1-Perhaps at the off there was an omnific ether,

Was it divine? Will that decide on what happened next?
My guess is as good as yours;
The Lord invented special effects,
(Rainbows and storms).

2-Is the law set in stone?

Do you like to have a moan?
Moses got a note, God spoke.
Some say the law is made for 'One Love'.
Noah sent out a dove,
An olive branch came back,
We suppose the bird had had her snack.
Is it fair to say that you and me
Want the truth to set us free?
Where would we all be?
If only we could see.

3-Every time a word is spoken,

There is a token shared,
Words from heaven never shrivel,
Look within, transcend the drizzle.
Every time a breath is taken,

Shaken, not stirred,
It is true that some are forsaken,
If they breathe ill will to the core shaken!

4-When a few points are scored,

The feelings of losing are ignored,
The point of winning is manifold,
It could be to turn effort into spiritual gold.

5-Tasty food's available from Mother Earth.

What we learn in school is priceless in worth.
Bountiful food is available to cook,
Take a look at recipe books.
In the kitchen, we try all our techniques,
To create something that tastes unique.
Our lessons learnt hold us in good stead,
Until we reach heaven rested, rested.

6-We never really, truly die,

Mystics tell us with words that fly,
Our spirit lives on if we believe,
Faith must be kept for us to achieve.

7-The end of daylight robbery,

Is the beginning of a mind that is free.
When we live carefully and carefree,
Our minds can be stilled in equanimity.

8-Of all the places to find peace,

Look within and exercise, for release.
Seek extra-curricular activities,
And get busy with feelings of ecstasy.

9-War is stopped by resolution.
There is no other solution.
Rest and look beyond the peace,
Elysian is where you'll enjoy the feast.

10-Something out of heaven could be a rhyme,

Like the first clock that ticked the time,
Although the perception of time is relative,
Patience is a virtue, a gift that gives.

11-Of all the places to look in a quest or task,

Sometimes the answer is found in one last gasp.
Solutions to problems are often found,
When we keep our ears clean with silence the sound.

12-Isn't it amazing this universe of ours,

The way it was created by super-cosmic powers?
From an ant to an elephant and garden flowers,
Solar storms could be the end of it all in hours.

13-A little is enough if a little is what you need.

A lot is not enough if you follow your greed.
Enjoyed every second or found it a bore,
I leave you now with one more verse to explore…

14-Good will comes from peacekeepers' hearts,

Blessed they are with care that lasts.
The world is in trouble, what do we need,
To plant more kindness so kindness breeds.
Hope you enjoyed these words,
Be free as eagles fly.

12. Liebestraum

(Dream of Love in Love's Dream)

Let each moment of love's dream eternally
Be sown,
So Liebestraum loves dance of love
Can dream inside of thee,
Chorus of wind song filled the evening,
As air continued delightful weaving,
Enjoyable to write to pleasure calm,
Travelling inner Liebestaum;
Colourful, colourful, Liebestraum!
TO PEACE

**Book 2
Ruminations**

For the old faith in a new hope…
'Muses from the inner and the outer realms of mind; dedicated to those who believe in hope, chips and 'the way of dipping in!'
Enjoy the dip.

I
First lines float
Comfortably on pages
Ducklings dip into a pond

II
With humility
Comes freedom dawning
Peace grows aplomb

III
Today's song-singing
For tomorrow's joy
Time is not let down

IV
Moving towards future
Away from past, present sits
Content as a cloud

V
What we create lives
Our imagination breathes
Goodness grows wings

VI

Equanimity stems from a haven

Happiness nurtured within

Who senses this

VII

Is the good life free

Once you take away the fee

For shelter, food and glee

VIII

When the cat passes

Clear pathways

Subtle spells spin

IX

Light enters the fray

Illuminating the room

Tea is sipped peppermint warm

X

Days come, good and bad

Contentment is when we are

Living beside compassion

XI

Summer merging

Seems to bring out the mixtures

Rain and shine

XII

Sometimes the weather

Breathes cold blasts of gusty winds

Feeling her is magical

XIII

Swaying branches move

Elegantly, gently, patiently

Willows flex, oaks groan

XIV

Circular breathing

Swirls and gushy as words

Failing and tumbling down

XV

Oceans without shores

Water without base

Inspiration lives

XVI

Never did a fool

Live in perfect harmony,

Unlike sage and rosemary

XVII

Words can spread

Butter on bread slices

To one and to all

XVIII

When peace is present

Inside alert minds

Let us share grace

To peace

Book 3
Journey to Eternity

1
Words through air speak volumes to one and all,
Sentiments are often sweet, short whispers sensitively small,
"I Love You" can create an early, premature curtain call,
Forever remembering, never deny her stall,
(the folly of lust versus love),
Love is the key to the door, never failing,
Speaks a truth that never lies,
Words never lying were always befriending ending in a smile, then a laugh, then a sigh.
(Relationships sail away into the Caribbean blue, sometimes never to be seen or heard again.)

2
Two hearts acting as one,
Life together beginning a song,
Is there anything remotely as strong?
To fight off any clanging gong?
Mega enough to pacify the throng,
Sometimes right, sometimes wrong,
Repelling all the chaos,
Fuss is a must to create love dust,
Cheese and crackers, inside lovers' trust,
As long as the song-of-songs continues manifest, intangible, impossible to rust.

3
Beauty may be in the eye of the beholder.
Make love based on feelings, not a splash or an odour.
Happiness inside the heart of love,
Building nests for chick doves.

Mute swans mate for life, that is true.
Empathy is utilised for the rest or the few.
A mole, a hair, a shrew – is this a test about birds with breasts?
If so, it just won't do.
(Many a time, the difference between love and lust is sobriety, not a dirty flirty second of desire set free in wild fires.)

4

Love can create ordinary miracles,
Cliqued yet somewhat funny.
A safe bet is to name your empire hive and find yourself a honey.
Love exists in the mind of humankind,
Well, for everyone who truly believes it can.
Never be envious of other people in love.
Your time will come when you least expect it to.
So 'they say' whether straight or nay,
To every woman or man with respectful hue.

5

Faith and friendship are the vehicles that drive communities.
Obtuse examples lead to cruelty.
A cute face may not last infinity.
Though with equilateral views, you get the equality.
Find and try what suits the unity best equally without futility.
(Shapely sense of humour I think you will agree.)

6

Love is transcendent and noble when harvested.

7

"Love is a gift that keeps on giving, being in love is winning."

(This line featured on a key fob 'favour' at my brother Michael and his beloved Jasmine's wedding day reception. Everyone at the reception received a gift with the verse on it – cool).

8

Love can mend a broken heart,
Melting cold, bitter souls.
Wake up, people, the time is here; forget about the ultimate fear.
To die alone in a state of empty-knowing,
Surrounded with no one dear,
Selfish swimming in the life for one,
No way to be considered someone fun.
Run with the wind, talk to the dogs, call upon a thousand frogs.
The most certain personage to call upon is above.
(Heaven is above us and the Kingdom of Heaven is within, so all we need to honestly do is learn to let go and let God in.)

9

When love enters the heart strings, music begins to play a symphony of devotion.

10

Of all the things in the world to possess,
Priceless in nature love's unpurchased.
Love is more than things that cause stress,
At the mountain peak of desire eustress.

11

Finally, the verses come to a close, and the door is about to shut.
Put the expressions to use or toss them in the bin; am I being too abrupt?
All I can say as a scribe once said, a long, long time ago,
The pen is mightier than the sword, and so I leave with these passing words in tow,

Love those close to you, both family and friends,

We may be strangers, and then again, perhaps one day our words may meet in…

The End

Book 4
Smashed And Rebuilt
A—Z Z—A

A

Here are the first three liner,

Hope you like her,

Experienced by trial and error.

B

There is a voice following me around.

Sometimes I think it might be you;

That would be so cool.

C

Little baby crying while sister is book-searching,

Mother minding all options.

Librarian hovers, dandelion-like.

D

Mindlessness is delusion; open the bottle,

Then there is an understanding that we are all so close,

Close to creating the ultimate connection.

E

Worry not, my friend, the time is now.

Time for what I hear you say?

To be aware of today and tomorrow, yesterday.

F

Blame the beauty on your grace,

Face to make us smile,

Forever you shine amazing.

G

Smashed, broken, crunched, destroyed,

Just a bottle dropped on the floor,

Open up another and drink on.

H

Love is a labyrinth.

Becoming attractive guides us to the core.

The core is pure; pure in spirit wins.

I

Inner virtues are the tastiest to eat.

Sometimes they are rare, other times common.

Rare virtues are worth seeking.

J

Stones are skimmed on deep oceans.

Noble is the ocean; shallow is skimming.

Dive deep to find the pearl.

K

Are you happy?

So happy you don't know what to do?

Find someone sad, give them love.

L

Mystery is only nonsense if it is unknown.

If known, it becomes divine.

If divine, ask no question.

M

Discover yourself; feel the fear.

Transform what is far into something near.

Nothing wrong lasts that long; be strong.

N

All the misery in the world equals pain.

You are all your pain; what is the time?

Half-past nine.

O

Spiders crawl innocently enough,

Then man shoves it on the fire.

Is that fair, mankind?

P

Excite with personality,

Stun with a look that never ends,

After a moment, smile and go away as friends.

S

Sweetness of nature always finds a home.

A sweet home is a hive of honey.

Where there is a honey, be sweet.

T

Beasts are small and great, gentle and wild,

Children are small and gentle.

Great and wild is life yet tamed.

U

Peace can be found in a nutshell,

If you like walnuts, that is.

Nutshells litter a squirrel's layer.

V

Spiritual truth is common sense.

Common is for everyone.

This truth is a sensible sense.

W

Fools eat all day and still hunger.

Wise ones are subtle.

If you don't like a grape, don't eat one.

X

Fun is as fun does.

Cool is as one believes.

Shalom is a state of mind mixed up in form.

Y

So, poetry, what's that all about?

Words, rhyme, messages,

A soul massage.

Z

Walking into a lamppost may hurt.

It doesn't compare to a broken heart,

Movement towards freedom.

Jason Christopher McLean aka Mishmashaton